MICROSOFT
PUBLISHER
365

An Updated Practical Guide for Beginner and Advanced Users

EVELYN NEUMANN

TABLE OF CONTENT

INTRODUCTION *6*

CHAPTER ONE *7*

EXPLAINING PUBLISHER *7*

 Choosing A Template 7

 Creating a Publication 10

 Restructuring a Publication 13

 Selecting a different template 14

 Selecting a color scheme 15

 Selecting a font scheme 17

CHAPTER TWO *19*

Setting up your pages *19*

 Obtaining a Better View of Your Work 20

 Moving from page to page 21

 Viewing single pages and two-page spreads 22

 Zooming in and out 22

 Understanding and using the Layout Guides 23

 Margin guides 23

 Grid guides 24

 Ruler guides 27

 Baselines 27

 Aligning objects to grid and ruler lines 28

CHAPTER THREE *29*

Purifying a Publication *29*

 Entering Text on the Pages 29

Entering text directly inside a page in Publisher without using a Word document 30

Making Text Fit in Text Frames 31

Fitting overflow text in a single frame 31

Making text flow from frame to frame 33

Making Text Wrap around a Frame or Graphic 36

CHAPTER FOUR 38

Swapping the Placeholder Pictures 38

Inserting Frames on the Pages 39

Inserting a new frame 39

Inserting a text-box frame 39

Inserting a table 41

Inserting a picture 43

Altering the size and position of frames 46

Inserting Pages 48

Removing a Page 50

Moving a page 51

CHAPTER FIVE 52

Putting on the Finishing Touches 52

Beautifying the Text 52

Methods for Beautifying Pages 60

Pugging in a page part 60

Investigating with borders and accents 64

CHAPTER SIX 68

Taking Benefit of Attention Getters 68

Background for pages 72

Master Pages for Dealing with Page Backgrounds............................ 75

Switching to the Master Page view 75

Running the Design Checker 76

Saving Your Publication 79

Printing a Publication 82

CONCLUSION *84*

INTRODUCTION

Microsoft Publisher is an astonishing tool that can help businesses in constructing newsletters, and visitation cards such as birthday cards, wedding cards, season cards, and other marketing materials. The publisher is a desktop publishing and layout application aspect of the Microsoft Office suite. Publishers can be used to produce and design professional-looking marketing and communication documents such as posters, flyers, and brochures. It is also directed at schools, home users, and small enterprises, publisher is not used for commercial printing tenacities. The reason for Microsoft Publishers is to provide users with a tool for producing professional quality communication and marketing materials, it also offers amazing templates and features that can make it easy to generate and design a greater document. Inside this mini book, you will be learning some of the things below:

- Creating a publication
- Redesigning a publication
- Obtaining a better view of your work
- Entering text on the pages
- Making text fit in text frames
- Decorating Text
- Inserting pictures, and table, and using Page parts
- Inserting borders and accents
- Using attention-getters, advertisements, and a lot more.

The Publisher is dissimilar from Microsoft Word in a way that the importance is positioned on page design and layout rather than text composition and proofreading. You can create numerous types of publications by making use of Publisher.

CHAPTER ONE

EXPLAINING PUBLISHER

Most people call a Publisher "a print shop in a can" because the application is very good at creating manufactured business cards, brochures, calendars, posters, newsletters, resumes, and so on. To do this there are many templates on Publisher that you make use of. Each template offers you with a pre-design calendar, brochure, and so on.

Choosing A Template

You can locate an appropriate template for any kind of publication you want to create. Templates entail placeholders for graphics and text. Kindly follow the steps below to choose a template for creating a publication:

1. **Enter Publisher in the search bar to unlock the Publisher interface then select publisher**

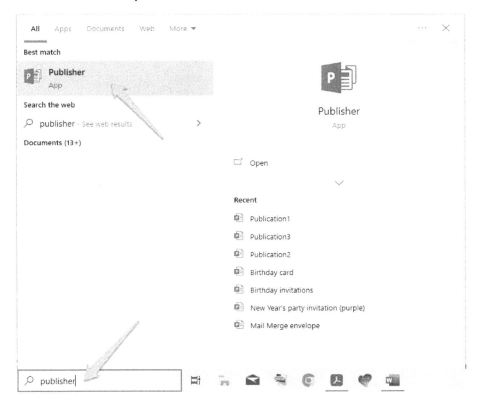

2. Select New from the navigation pane.

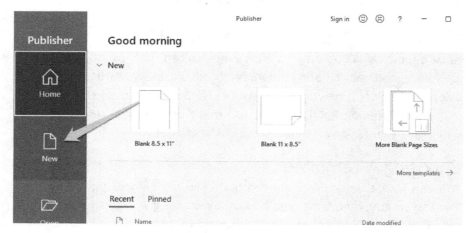

3. Then pick a template.

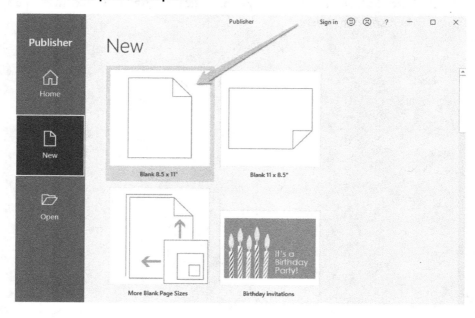

Immediately you pick a template the publisher's home screen will come into sight. See the image below:

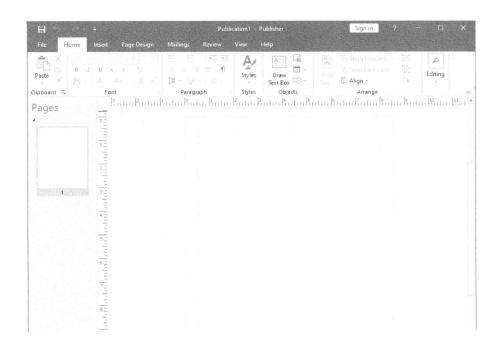

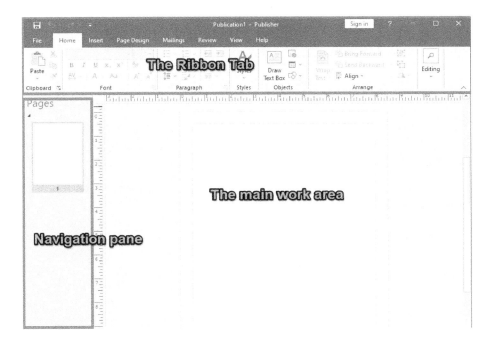

Creating a Publication

To create a new publication, follow the steps below

1. **Visit the File tab**

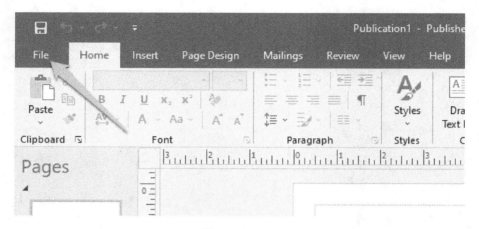

2. **Then select New or press Ctrl+N**

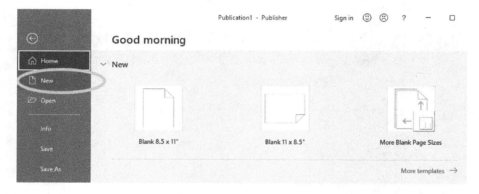

The New window appears, where you can create a publication with any of these methods:

➢ **Select a built-in template:** On the Built-in tab, choose the icon representing a category (Business Cards, Brochures, and so on) you see numerous templates. Navigate through the list, choose a template, and click Create. See the image below:

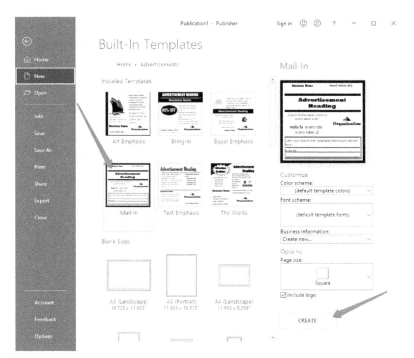

➢ **Search online for a template:** On the Office tab, in the Search for Online Templates text box, input the name of a publication type and click the Start Searching button or press Enter.

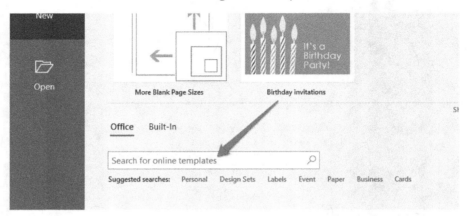

Choose a category and click a template to investigate it in a preview screen. Click the Create button to create a publication.

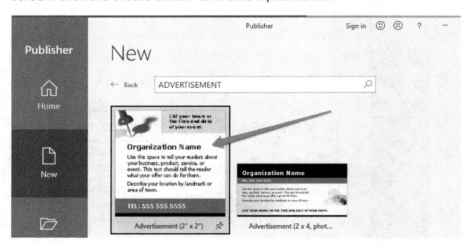

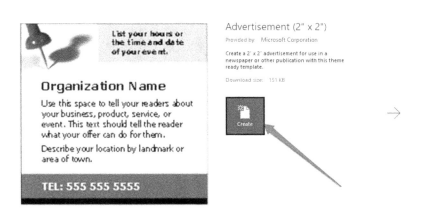

Restructuring a Publication

You can modify publication designs, color schemes, and so on. To restructure a publication, visit the Page Design tab, and design options.

This tab provides chances for changing or altering templates, the orientation and size of pages, font schemes, and color schemes. See the image below:

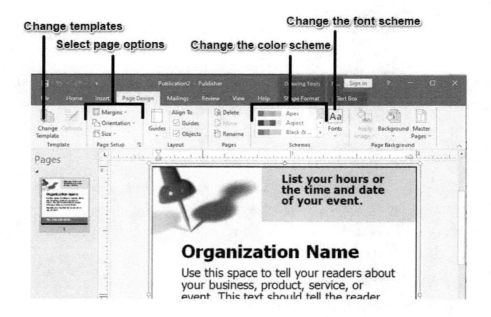

Selecting a different template

If you are not satisfied with the template you selected when you created your Publication, to replace it with a new one, visit the Page Design and click the Change Template button.

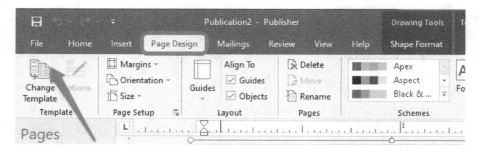

The Change Template window appears, where you can choose a different template. see the image below:

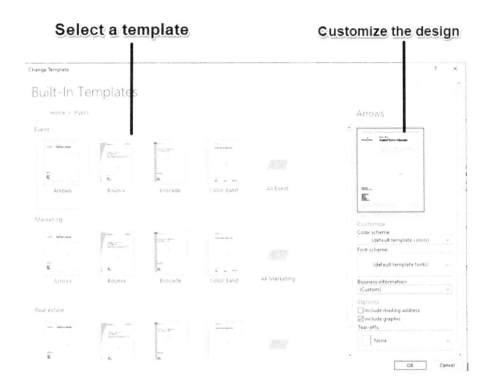

Selecting a color scheme

To select a different color scheme for your publication, visit the Page Design tab and choose a scheme in the Schemes gallery.

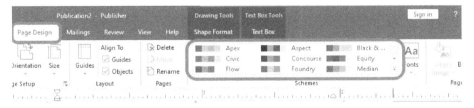

You can also pick Create New Color Scheme at the bottommost of the gallery and fashion your color scheme in the Create New Scheme dialog box. To do this, Click the downward arrow. Pick Create New Color Scheme.

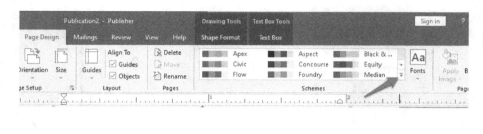

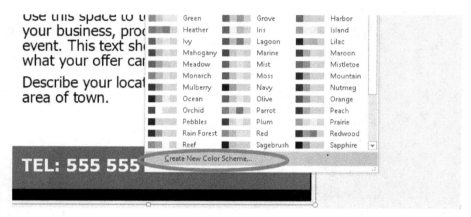

The Create scheme dialog box appears

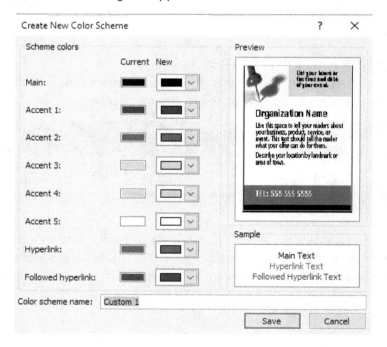

Selecting a font scheme

Most of the text formats that are available in Microsoft Word can also be found in Microsoft Publisher on the Home tab. To boldface text, choose the text and click the Bold button. to modify font sizes, select an option on the Font Size drop-down menu.

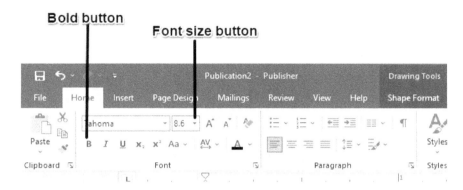

If you want to avoid the stress of formatting text, you can select a **font scheme** or a pair of fonts for the headings and body text in a publication. Font scheme saves you from the problem of having to format the text on your own. To select a font scheme, follow the steps below:

 ➢ **Click the Page Design tab**
 ➢ **Click the Fonts button**
 ➢ **Then choose a scheme on the drop-down menu.**

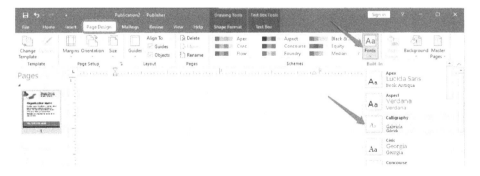

You can also choose Create New Font Scheme on the drop-down menu and pick fonts for heading text and body text in the dialog box that displays.

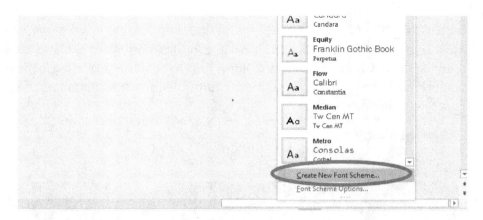

See the Create New Font Scheme dialog box below.

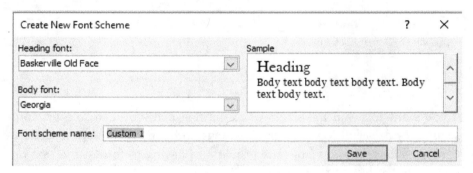

CHAPTER TWO

Setting up your pages

To set up your pages, visit the Page Design tab to regulate the margin size, orientation, and page size of your publication:

> ➤ **Margins:** Click the Margins button and select an option on the drop-down menu or click Custom Margins to enter margin measurements in the Layout Guides dialog box.

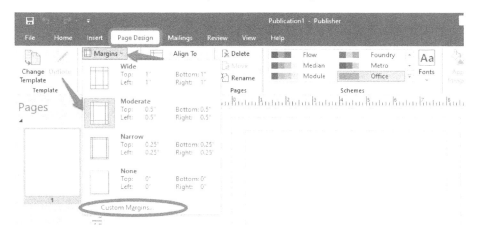

> ➤ **Orientation:** Click the Orientation button and select Landscape or Portrait on the drop-down menu to stand your publication upright to turn it on its side.

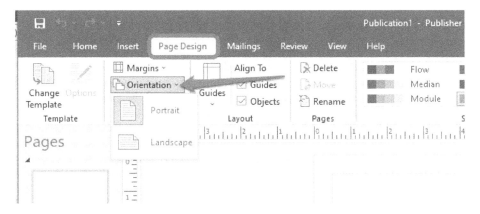

➢ **Size:** Click the Size button and choose a page size on the drop-down menu, you can also select Create New Page Size in the list to unlock the Create New Page Size dialog box and affirm a page size of your own.

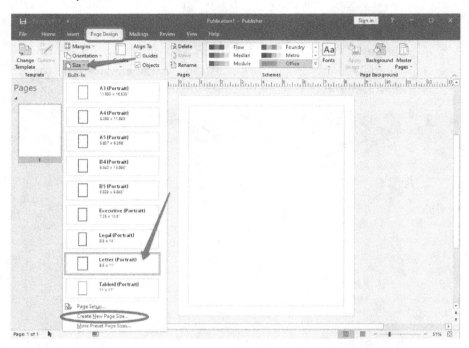

Obtaining a Better View of Your Work

Publisher provides numerous tools for changing or modifying views of your work. The image below displays what these tools are. They are explained in the following pages.

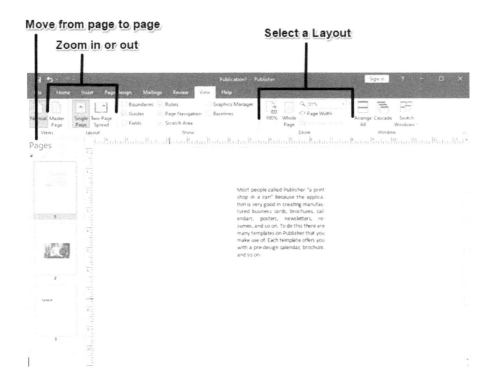

Moving from page to page

Apply these methods to navigate from page to page in a publication:

> **Pages pane:** In a Publication that has more than one page, move from page to page by clicking thumbnail pages in the Pages pane, to do this, click the View tab then click the Page Navigation check box. See the image above.

> **The Go To Page dialog box:** On the Home tab, unlock the drop-down menu on the Find button and select Go To Page. Then impute a page number in the Go To Page dialog box.

See the Go To Page dialog box image below

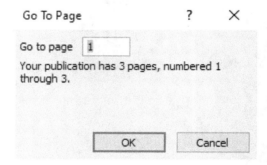

Viewing single pages and two-page spreads

On the View tab, click the Two-Page Spread button to view facing pages in brochures, newsletters, and other publications with more than one page. Selecting this command early and frequently. It allows you to view what readers of your publication will see when they view facing pages. Select the Single Page button to view a single page in the window.

Zooming in and out

Aside from the standard Zoom controls found in most Office programs. The publisher provides numerous commands for zooming in or out. Visit the View tab and take benefit of these methods as you enhance your publication:

➢ **Make the width of the page fit in the window:** Click the Page Width button.

- ➢ **Make the page fit squarely in the window:** Click the Whole Page Button to make the entire page fit in the window.
- ➢ **View your publication at its actual size:** Click the 100% button.
- ➢ **Focus on objects:** Choose an object, for instance, a text frame or graphic, or many objects and click the Selected Objects button to zoom in on what you chose.

Understanding and using the Layout Guides

It is essential to make graphics, frames, and lines of text line up squarely on the page if your publication is to look smart and snappy. Publisher provides numerous types of layout guides, as the following pages describe.

Margin guides

Margin guides are blue lines that display where page margins begin and stop. Margin guides show on the page as long as the Guides check box on the View tab is chosen. where the margin guides appear to rely on the Margin setting you selected for your publication. Click the Margins button and choose a setting, on the Page Design tab.

Grid guides

Grid guides are blue lines that display in grid form all over the page see the image below:

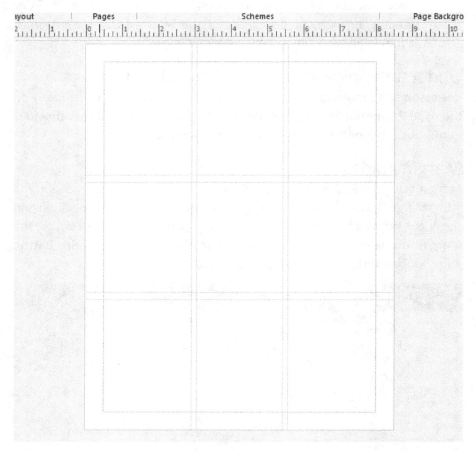

To determine where gridlines are and appear on pages, kindly follow the steps below.

1. Click the Page Design tab
2. Click the Guides button
3. Select Grid and Baseline Guides on the drop-down menu.

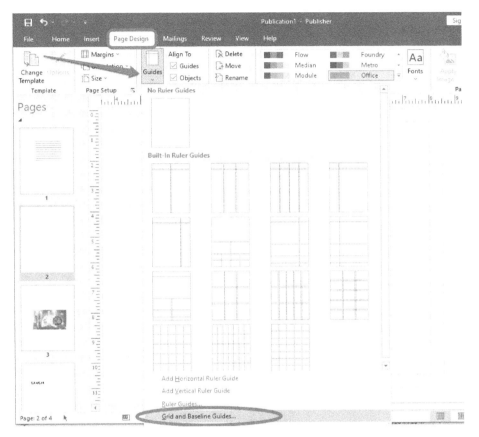

The Grid Guides tab of the Layout Guides dialog box appears, as displayed below.

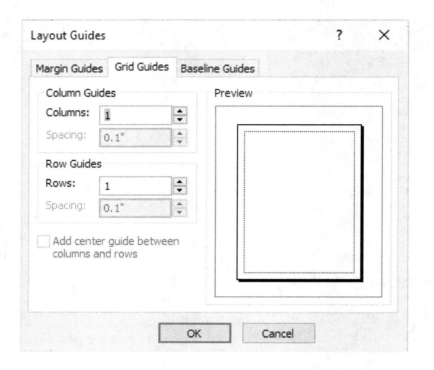

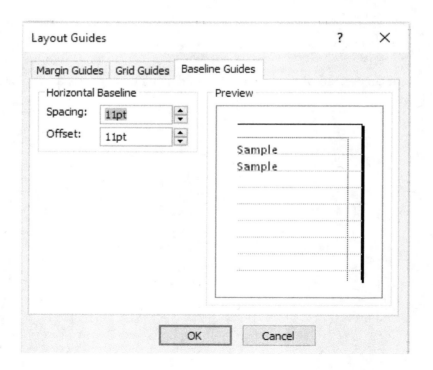

Do the following and click OK:

> ➢ Impute numbers to fix how many rows and columns form the grid.
> ➢ Enter Spacing measurements to regulate how close objects can come to grid guides.
> ➢ Choose the Add Center Guide between Columns and Rows check box if you want to draw a line between the lines formed by columns and rows in the grid.

To delete grid guides, visit the View tab and deselect the Guides check box to delete grid guides temporarily.

Ruler guides

Ruler guides are green horizontal and vertical lines that you can place on the page for help in aligning objects and frames. Visit the Page Design tab and use one of these methods to position ruler guides on a page:

> ➢ **Ruler Guides dialog box:** Click the Guides button and select Ruler Guides. The Ruler Guides dialog box appears. Impute horizontal or vertical measurements for the guides then click OK.
> ➢ **Drawn ruler guides:** Click the Guides button and select Add Horizontal Ruler Guide or Add Vertical Ruler Guide. A ruler guide comes into sight Horizontally or vertically over the middle of the page. Click and drag the ruler guide over the page to a new place.
> ➢ **Built-in ruler guides:** Click the Guides button and select a built-in ruler guide option on the drop-down list to position several ruler guides on a page.

Baselines

Baselines are brown, horizontal, dotted lines that display on the page to assist with aligning objects, frames, and lines of text. To make a baseline display, visit the View tab and choose the Baselines check box.

To determine the frequency of baselines, visit the Page Design tab, click the Guides button, and select Grid and Baseline Guides on the drop-down menu. You see the Guides dialog box, on the Baseline Guide tab, impute Spacing measurements to decide how tight or loose the lines are, and also impute Offset measurements to decide how far off the margin settings the lines are.

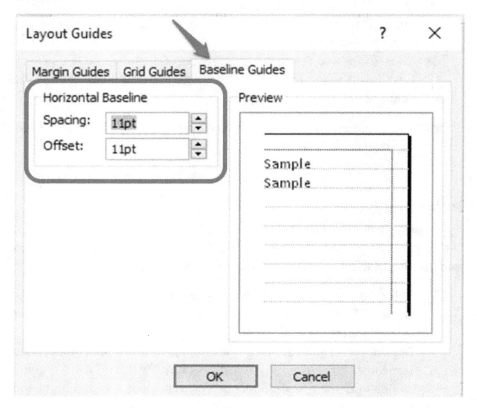

Aligning objects to grid and ruler lines

On the Page Design tab, the commands in the Layout group make frames and objects align to grid guides or ruler guides. Aligning aids to make objects line up squarely. On the Page Design tab, choose the Guides check box to make objects align to the guides; choose the Objects check box to make objects align to other objects on the page.

CHAPTER THREE

Purifying a Publication

This is the continuation of the previous chapters. In the previous chapters of this book, you discover how to create a publication, navigate your way around the screen, and use the diverse guides. In this chapter, you will discover how to make a publication your own. This chapter provides speed methods for entering and editing text. It also explains how to deal with frames, make text navigate from frame to frame, and insert graphics and other kinds of art in a publication.

Entering Text on the Pages

If you want to work on greeting cards, you have only a handful of words to write, you can write them in Publisher. But if you are working on a story, the easiest way to deal with the text is to write it in Word and import it. Kindly follow the instructions below to replace the placeholder text in a text frame with text from a Word document:

1. **Open a Word document, write the text, and save the text**

2. **In Publisher, Click on the placeholder text, move to the Home tab, click the Styles button, and note on the Styles drop-down list which style has been assigned to the placeholder text.**

3. **If necessary, press Ctrl+A to choose the text in the story.**

4. **On the Insert tab, click the Insert File button.** you see the Insert Text dialog box.

5. **Choose the Word file with the replacement text and click the OK button.**

6. **Press Ctrl+A to choose the text in the story, visit the Home tab, click the Styles button, and select the style that was allocated to the placeholder.**

Entering text directly inside a page in Publisher without using a Word document

This is another method of inserting text into a page in Publisher, kindly follow the steps below to insert text in a page:

1. **On the Home tab, click Draw Text Box.**

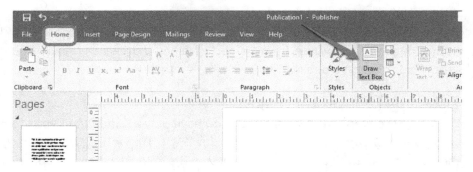

2. **Click on the page and drag the box that appears to your size.**

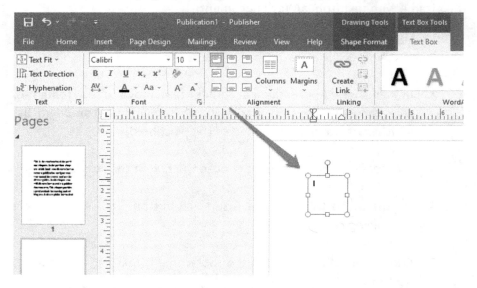

3. **Click in the text box and start typing.**

Making Text Fit in Text Frames

When text doesn't fit in a text frame, red selection handles display around the frame. The text in the Overflow icon is displayed in the lower-right corner of the text frame, see the image below:

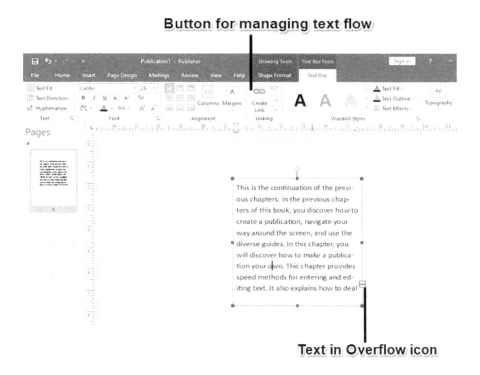

When you see this icon and the red selection handles, it means that you must make decisions on how to fit stray text into text frames. These pages describe strategies for dealing with text that doesn't fit in text frames.

Fitting overflow text in a single frame

To fit a paragraph or heading into a single text frame, apply one of these methods:

> ➤ **Edit the text:** Snip out a sentence or word here and there to make the text fit.

➢ **Make the text frame larger:** Click the frame to show the selection handles; then, drag a handle.

➢ **Shrink the text automatically:** On the Text Box tab, click the Text Fit button and select Shrink Text On Overflow on the drop-down menu.

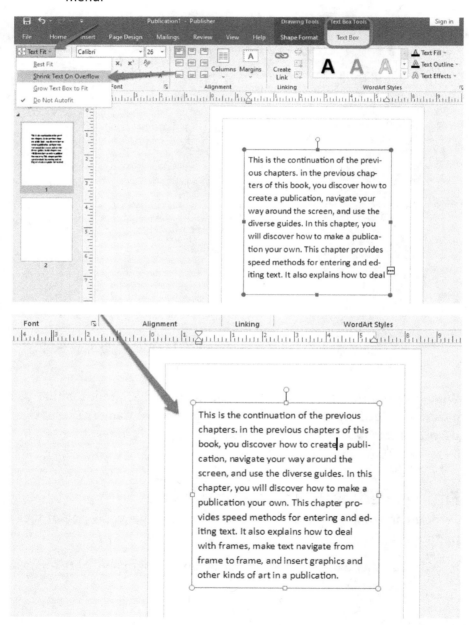

- ➢ **Make the text frame margins smaller:** Text frames have internal margins, like a page, to prevent text from getting too close to the frame border. To shrink these margins and make more space for text, visit the Text Box tab, click the Margins button, and select Narrow on the drop-down menu.

Making text flow from frame to frame

To make text flow from one frame to another, create a new text box for the overflow text and follow the instructions below:

- ➢ **Choose the text frame with overflowing text.**

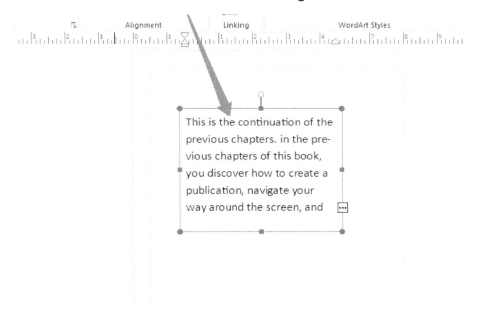

- ➢ **On the Text Box tab, click the Create Link button.**

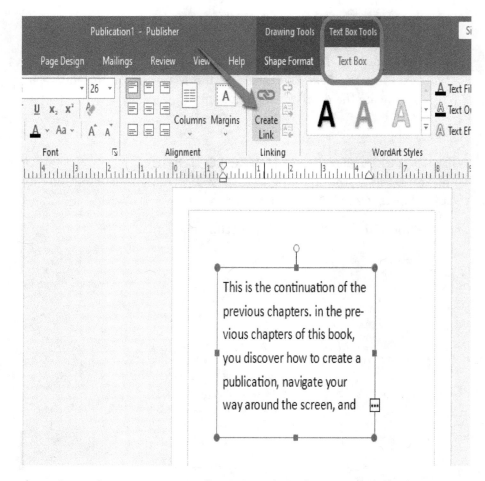

the pointer changes to an overflowing pitcher after you click the button.

➢ **Shift the pointer over the box that you want the text to flow into.**

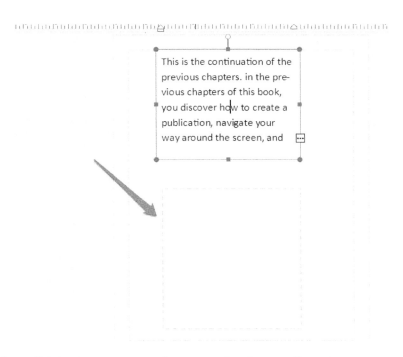

> **Click in the target text box to make the text flow there.**

Making Text Wrap around a Frame or Graphic

Wrap text around a frame, picture, or a WordArt image and you obtain an amazing layout, the picture below shows text that has been wrapped around an image.

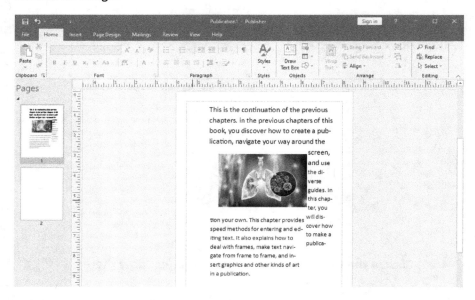

Below are instructions for wrapping text:

1. Choose the item that the text is to wrap around.

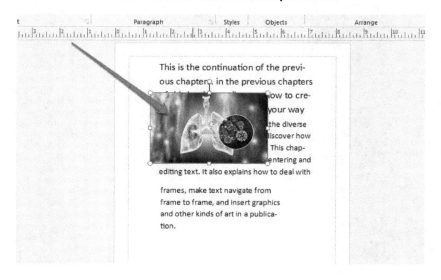

2. On the Format tab, click the Wrap Text button and select a wrapping option on the drop-down menu.

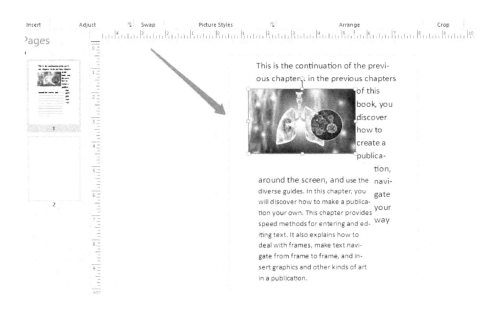

CHAPTER FOUR

Swapping the Placeholder Pictures

Apart from writing your word to replace the one already in a placeholder, you can also replace the generic pictures with your pictures.

Follow these instructions below to swap the placeholder picture with your picture:

1. **click the placeholder picture to choose it:**

   you can also choose a picture by clicking its name in the Graphics Manager. To apply the Graphics Manager, visit the View tab and pick the Graphics Manager check box. The Graphics Manager unlocks on the right side of the screen.

2. **Visit the Picture Format tab, click the Change Picture button, and select Change Picture on the drop-down menu.**

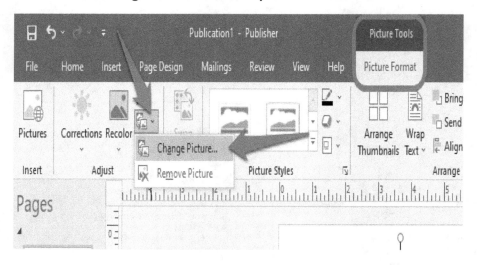

   The Insert Pictures screen comes into sight.

3. **Select From a File.**

   The Insert Picture dialog box appears.

4. **Choose a picture and click the Insert button.**

Inserting Frames on the Pages

Publications comprise frames such as text box frames, table frames, and picture frames. These pages describe all you need to know about frames.

Inserting a new frame

Inserting a new frame hang on what to insert: a table, picture, text box, or WordArt image. And to delete a frame all you need to do is pick the frame on the page then press the Delete key or right-click and select Delete Object.

Inserting a text-box frame

Follow the steps below to insert a text-box frame:

1. **Visit the Insert tab or Home tab.**

2. **Click the Draw Text Box button.**

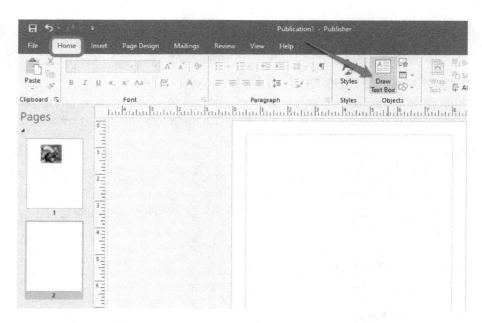

3. Then click the page and drag to create the text box.

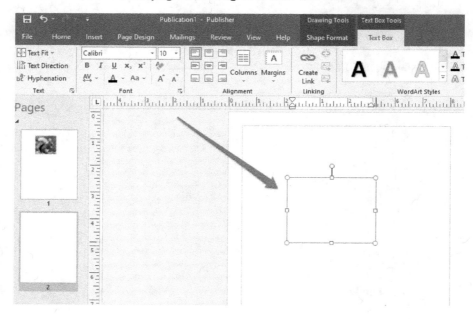

Inserting a table

To insert a table, visit the Home tab or Insert tab and apply one of these methods:

> ➢ Click the Table button and select Insert Table on the drop-down list. The Create Table dialog box displays. You can now input the number of rows and columns you want and click OK.

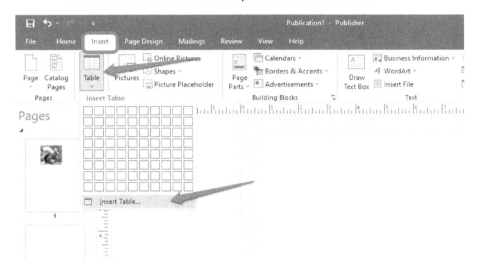

See the Create Table dialog box below.

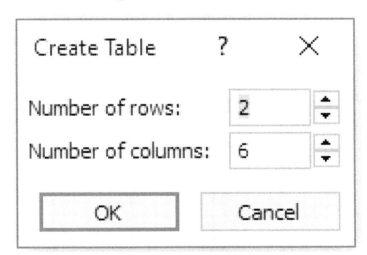

➤ Click the Table Button and move the pointer in the drop-down menu to the number of rows and columns you need. Release the mouse button or press Enter key.

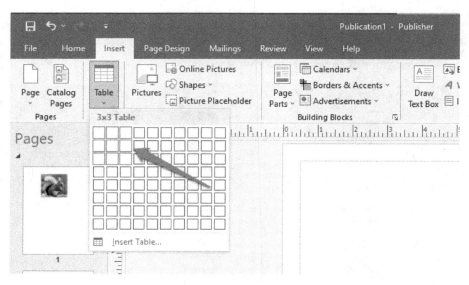

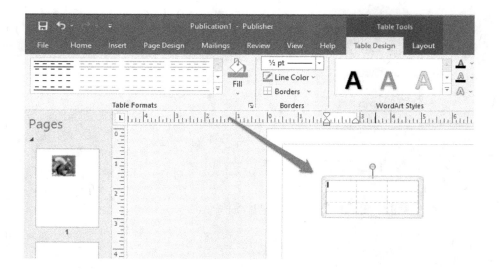

Inserting a picture

Follow the instructions below to insert a picture:

1. **Visit the Insert tab, and click the Picture Placeholder button.**

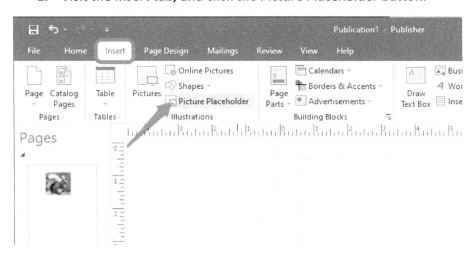

A picture placeholder frame appears on the page.

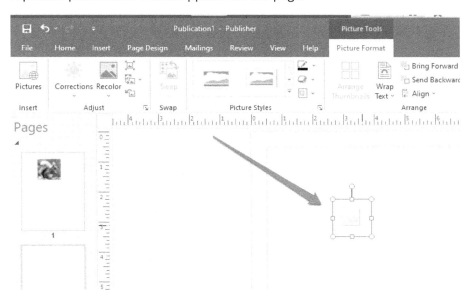

2. **Then resize the frame to the size you want your picture to be.** You can do this by dragging the resize handle

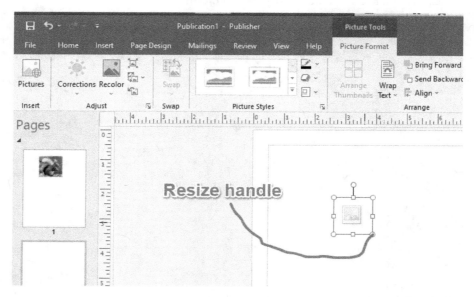

3. **Click the picture icon in the placeholder frame.**

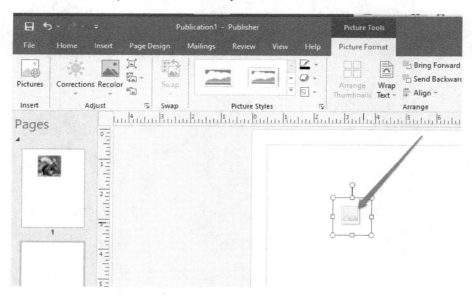

You might need the internet to insert pictures online or insert pictures without the internet by working offline. For me, I will click work offline.

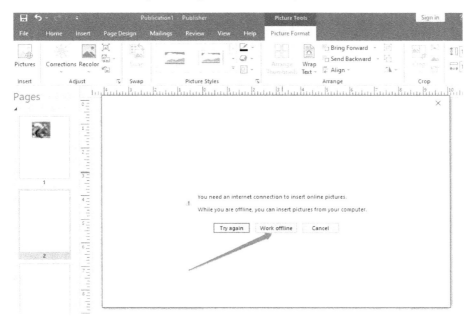

The Insert Pictures dialog box comes into sight.

4. Choose a picture and click the Insert button.

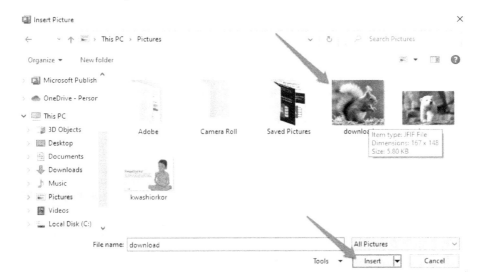

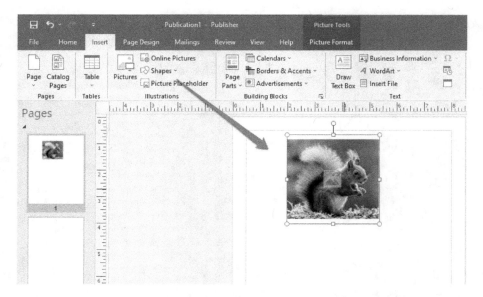

5. **Visit the Picture Format tab, and click the Fit button to make a picture that is too large or too small for the frame fit in the frame.**

Altering the size and position of frames

Apply these standard methods below for resizing and moving frames:

➤ **Altering the size of a frame:** Move the pointer across a selection handle and start dragging. See the image below:

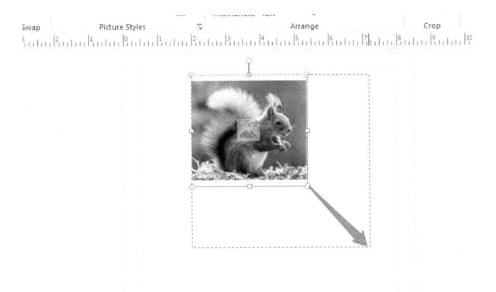

> **Altering the position of a frame:** Move the pointer onto the frame, and click and drag when you see the Four-headed arrow. To move more than one frame simultaneously, Ctrl+click the frames you want to move.

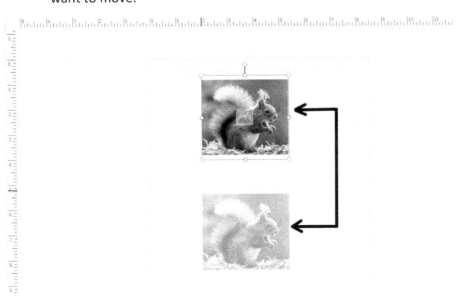

Inserting Pages

To insert a page, visit the Insert tab, click the Page button, and select an option on the drop-down list.

> **Insert Blank Page:** Selecting this option will insert an empty page.

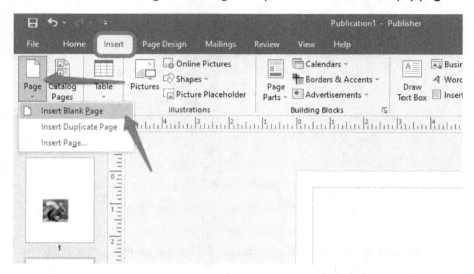

> **Insert Duplicate Page:** Picking this option will give you an identical page to the thumbnail page you selected.

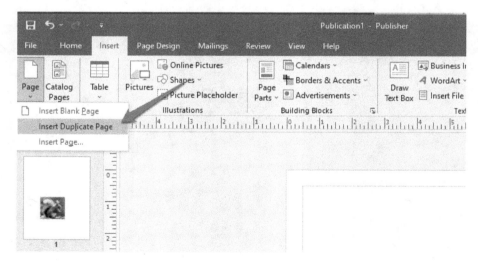

➤ **Insert Page:** Choose this option to unlock the Insert Pages dialog box, where you can enter the number of pages you want to insert and click the More button to put the new pages before or after the page you selected.

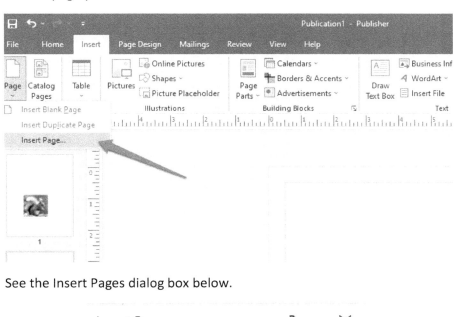

See the Insert Pages dialog box below.

Removing a Page

To remove a page, follow the steps below:

- Click the Page Design tab.
- Then click the Delete button.

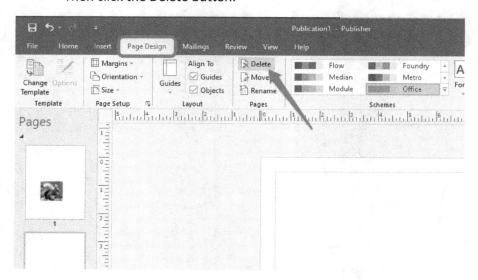

You can also right-click a page thumbnail and select Delete

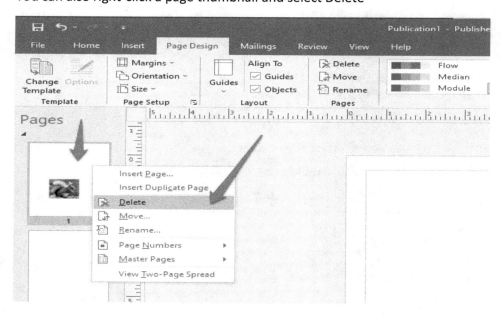

Moving a page

Kindly follow the steps below to move a page.

- Click the Page Design tab.
- Then Click the Move button.

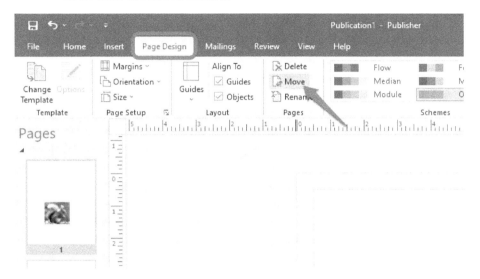

Give orders for moving the page in the Move Page dialog box and click OK. See the Move Page dialog box below:

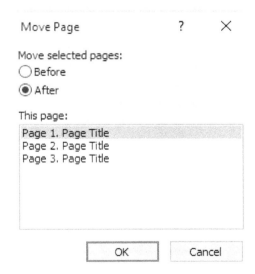

CHAPTER FIVE

Putting on the Finishing Touches

This chapter discovers drop caps and horizontal rules, page backgrounds and borders, borders, and backgrounds for frames, and how to place a logo in the same place on each page in a publication. It displays your Publisher's excellent Design Checker. This chapter also provides a few simple tricks for making publications more fashionable, and a lot more.

Beautifying the Text

Here are some tricks to amaze your friends and frighten your foes. These pages describe how horizontal rules and drop caps make a publication a little sparkling.

Drawing a horizontal rule on a frame

A horizontal rule is a horizontal line that divides one part of a page from another and guides the reader's eye on the page.

Choose the frame and follow the instructions below to draw a horizontal rule on a frame:

1. **Select the frame and click the Format tab.**

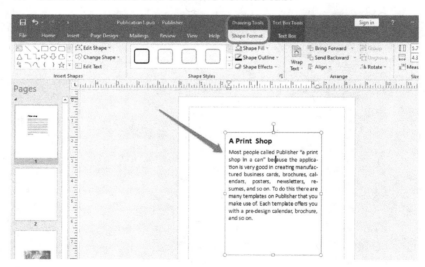

2. **Click the Text or Size group button, then visit the Color and Lines tab**

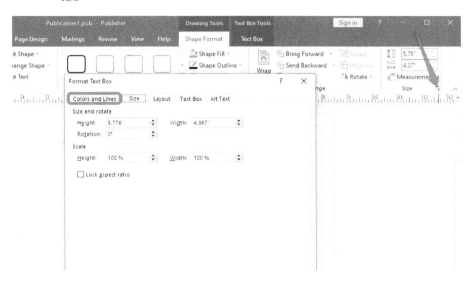

see the Color and Lines tab details below:

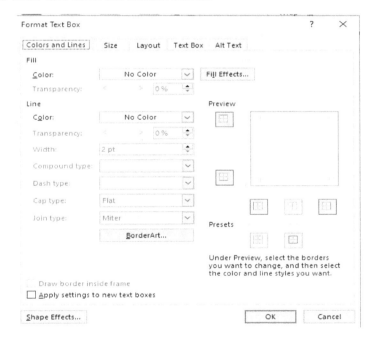

3. **In the Preview box, click the topmost of the box to draw a rule above the frame or the bottommost of the box to draw a rule below.**

By clicking part of the Preview box, you inform the Publisher where you want to draw the rule.

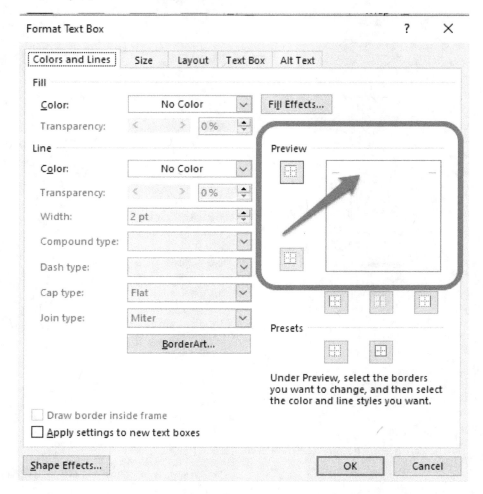

4. **On the Width menu, enter how wide you want the line to be in points.**

Observe the Preview box to view how wide the line is.

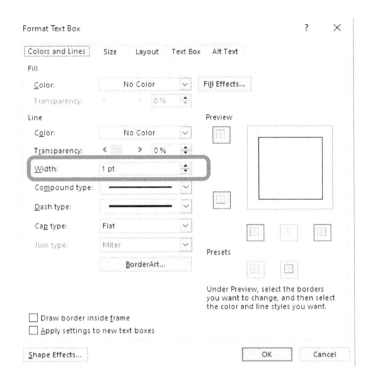

5. On the Compound Type menu, select the kind of line you want.

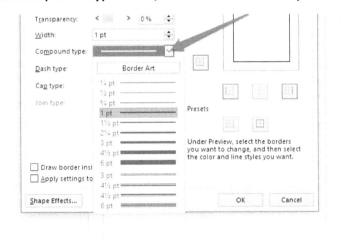

6. **Click again in the Preview box to draw a second rule on the frame, then repeat Steps 4 and 5.**
7. **Click Ok.** See the result below.

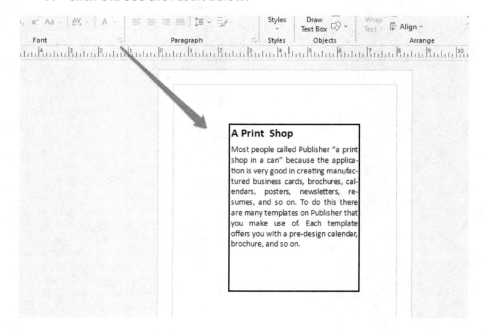

Dropping in a drop cap

A drop cap is a large capital letter that "drops" into the text. Drop caps are usually located in the first paragraph of a chapter or an article. Kindly follow the steps below to position a drop cap in a publication:

1. **Click the paragraph that needs a drop cap.**

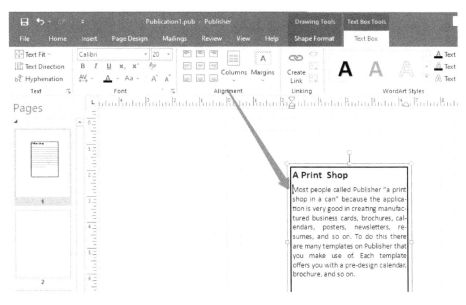

2. **Click the Text Box tab.**

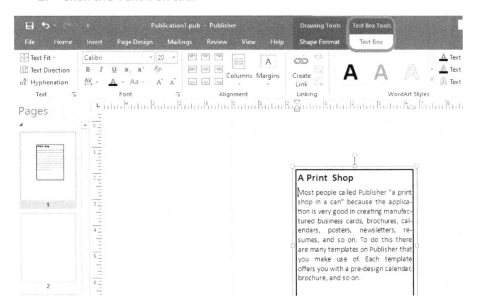

3. **Select the Typography button, and click the Drop cap button**

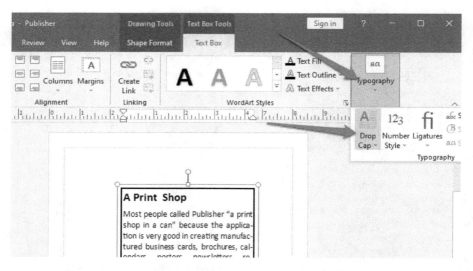

4. Then choose a drop cap from the drop-down list.

you can also select Custom Drop Cap to unlock the Drop Cap dialog box.

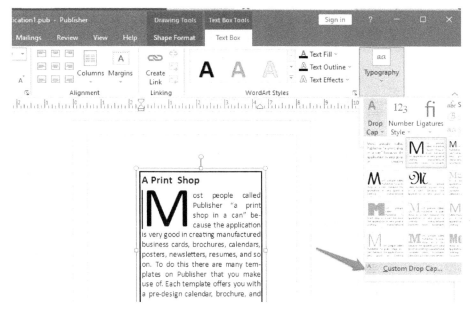

See the Drop Cap dialog box below:

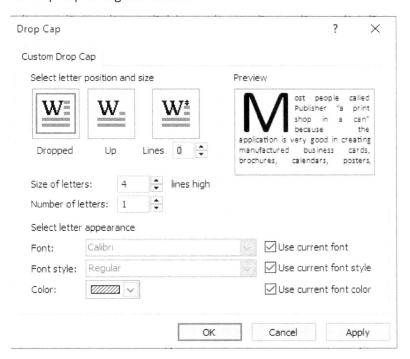

from here you select how far to drop the capital letter or choose a font and color for the letter.

Methods for Beautifying Pages

Below are the simple methods to make pages a little bit sparkling, No one likes a dull Publication. Continue reading to discover how to take advantage of page parts, accents, borders, and advertisements. You will also discover instructions for painting the whole page with a background color or gray shade.

Pugging in a page part

Page part is the Publisher's word for a page element that you quickly plug into a page. Apply a page part to fill in space on a page or get a head start in formatting part of a page. Page parts comprise the following:

> **Stories:** A preformatted story, comprising a heading and a subheading.
> **Pull quotes:** A preformatted text-box frame for showing a quotation from a story.
> **Headings:** A ready-made title for a page or story. Headings often comprise a subheading.
> **Sidebars:** A preformatted text-box frame for a cohort story.

Kindly follow the steps below to put a page part on a page:

1. **Click the page part button on the Insert tab.**

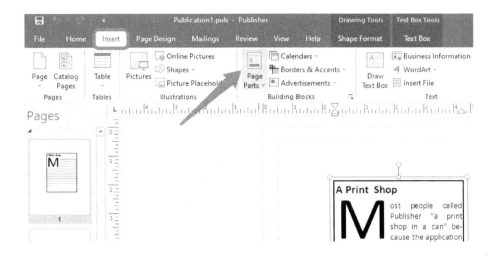

2. **Select a heading (sidebar, pull quote, or story) on the drop-down menu.**

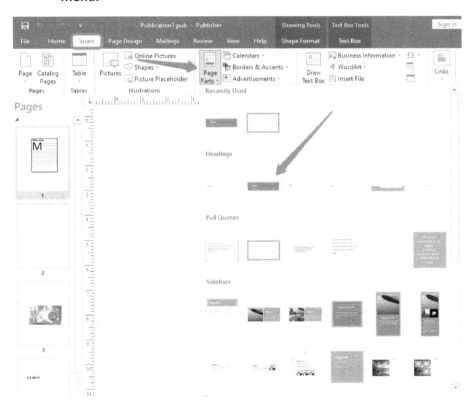

See the result below.

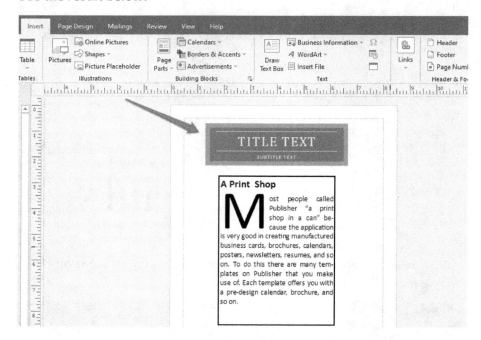

Select More Page Parts to unlock the Building Block Library and pick from numerous more page parts.

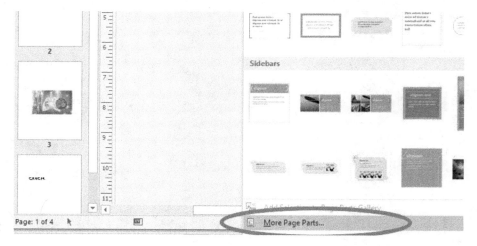

See the Building Block Library image below.

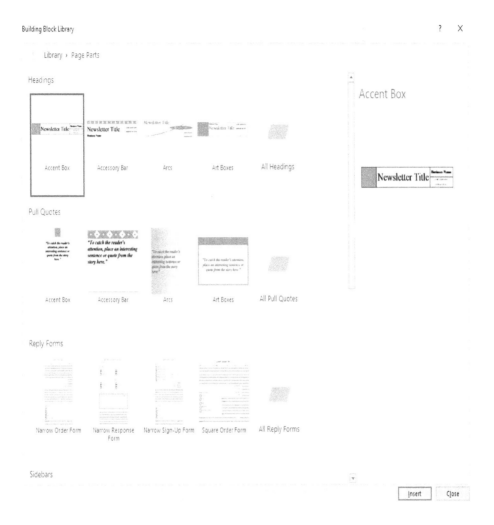

Immediately after the element appears on the page, you can change its size or move its position by applying the same methods you use with other objects. See the example of page parts below.

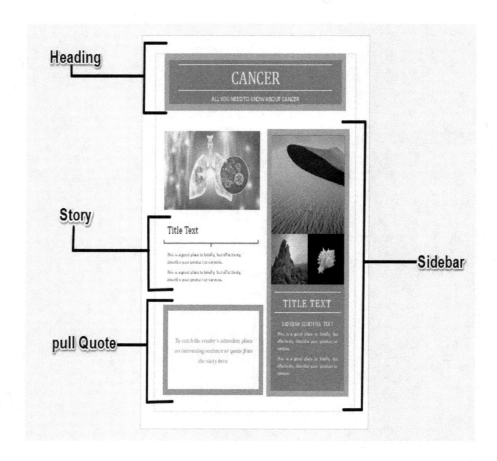

Investigating with borders and accents

Publisher provides what it calls **border and accents** to make pages a little sparkling. Borders and accents are page decorations that also serve a purpose:

- ❖ **Frames:** Four-sided text-box frames to make text boxes stand out.
- ❖ **Bars:** Attractive patterns for filling empty page space.
- ❖ **Emphasis:** Two-sided text-box frames to make text-boxes stand out on the page.
- ❖ **Patterns:** Checkerboard and other patterns for filling empty page space.
- ❖ **Lines:** Uncommon lines.

Follow these instructions to position a border or accent on a publication page:

1. On the Insert tab, click the Borders and Accents button.

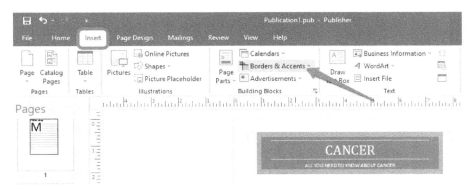

2. Select a border or accent on the drop-down menu.

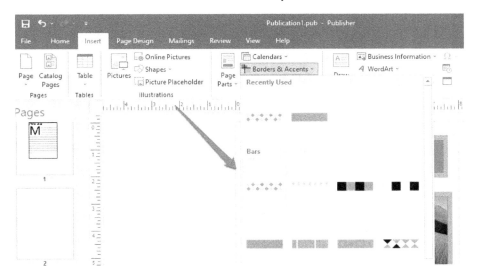

you can select More Borders and Accents and make a selection in the Building Block Library if you want to position a line or pattern on a page.

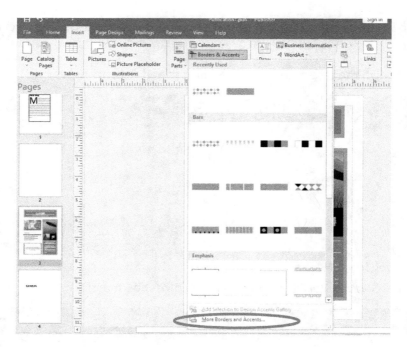

See the Building Block Library below.

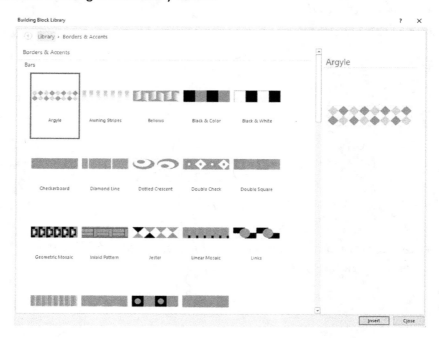

Make your selection and click the Insert button.

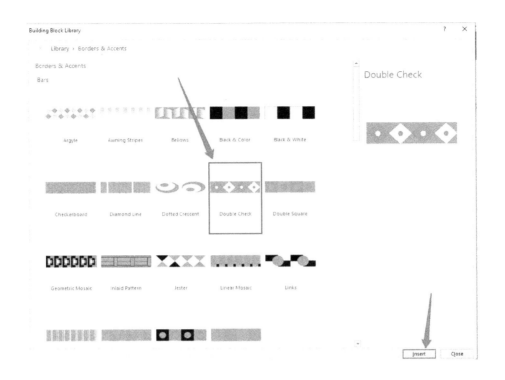

CHAPTER SIX

Taking Benefit of Attention Getters

This chapter is the continuation of the previous chapter. If your aim in Publisher is to create an advertisement, you can obtain a head start on the task by sprinkling an **attention-getter** or advertisement in your publication. In this final chapter, you will also discover how to save your publication in PDF format and how to print your publication. The image below shows examples of attention-getters.

To apply attention-getter or advertisement in your publication, follow the steps below:

1. **Click the Insert tab, then select the Advertisements button.**

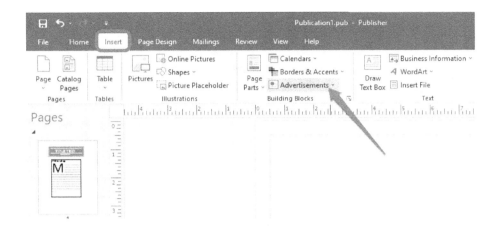

2. **Pick an advertisement or attention-getter on the drop-down menu.**

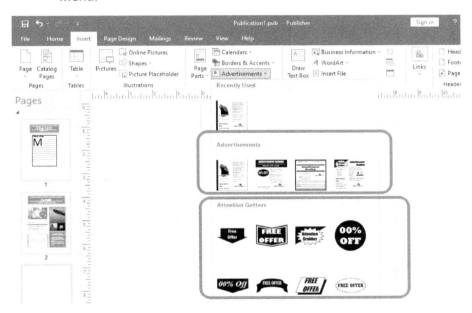

3. **Select More Advertisements on the drop-down list to unlock a dialog box with numerous advertisements and attention-getters.**

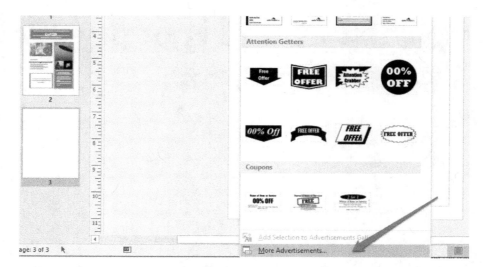

The dialog box appears.

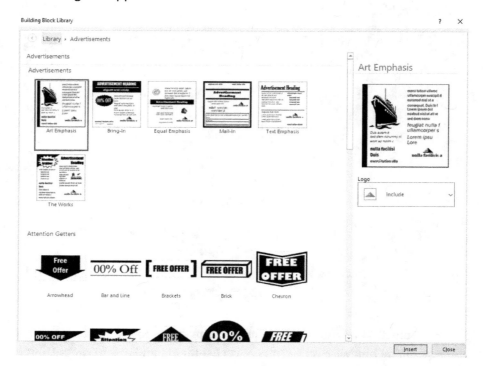

4. Pick anyone you like and click the insert button.

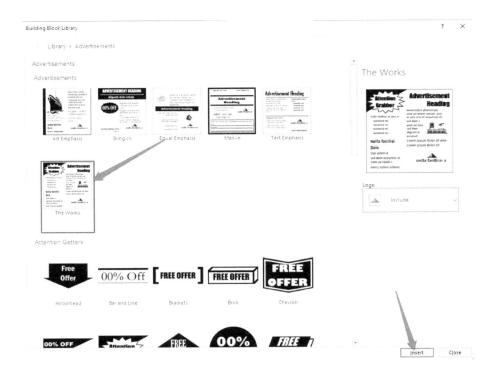

The advertisement will appear on the page immediately.

Background for pages

Another amazing trick is to place a color, gray shade, or other type of background on the page. Be certain to select a background that will not obstruct your publication or make it useless to read. Shrink the publication to 40% so that you can view what backgrounds look like; then follow these instructions below to give a page or the entire pages in your publication a background:

1. **Click the Page Design, then select the Background button.**

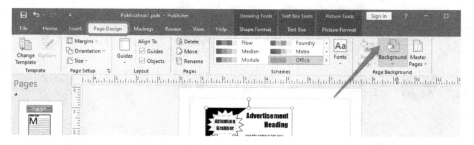

A drop-down list unlocks.

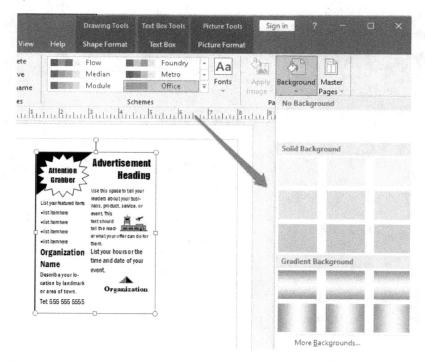

2. **Shift the pointer across the options on the drop-down list to live-preview the choices.**

   You can also select More Backgrounds on the drop-down menu to unlock the Format Background dialog box and select or create a page background there.

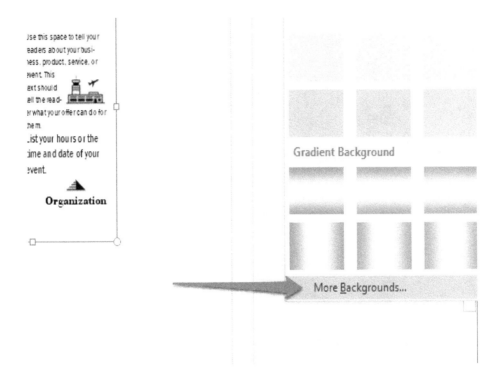

See the dialog box below.

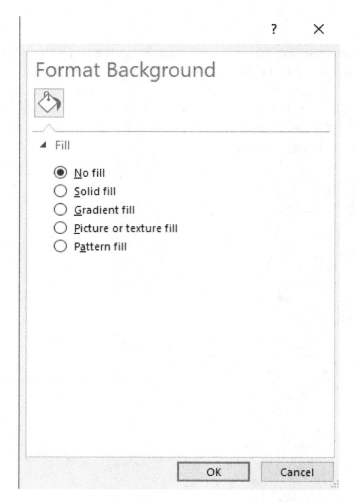

from here you can use a gradient, texture, pattern, or picture for a page background.

3. **Apply your choice to all pages or single pages in your publication.**

You have the option of modifying the page background on one page or the entire page:

- **One page:** On the Background button drop-down menu, right-click your choice and select Apply to Current Page.
- **All pages:** On the Background button drop-down menu, right-click your choice and pick Apply to All Pages.

Master Pages for Dealing with Page Backgrounds

In a publication with numerous pages, the same objects appear on every page. The good thing is that you do not need to position the objects on each page separately. Instead, you can position the objects on the **master page.** Whatsoever is on the master page displays on all pages in a publication. Below are instructions for dealing with master pages.

Switching to the Master Page view

To modify the appearance of the master page, position an object on the master page, and begin by switching to the Master Page view:

> ➤ **Click the Master Page button on the View tab.**

> ➤ **click the Page Design tab, then select the Master Pages button and pick Edit Master Pages on the drop-down menu.**

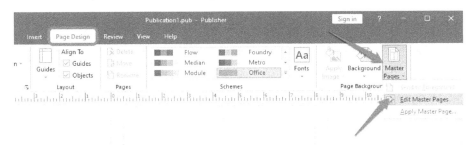

Visit the Master Page tab and click the Close Master Page button, to leave the Master Page view.

Running the Design Checker

When your publication is ready for printing, be certain to run the Design Checker. Kindly follow the steps below to run the Design Checker:

1. **click the file tab.**

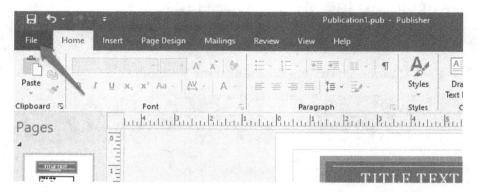

2. **click the info.**

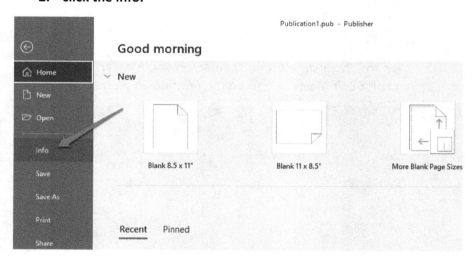

3. **Click the Run Design Checker button to run the Design Checker.**

The Design Checker task pane unlocks and lists items that need your attention. Unlock an item's drop-down menu and select Go to This Item to discover it in your publication. Sometimes the drop-down menu provides a rapid fix also. See the image below.

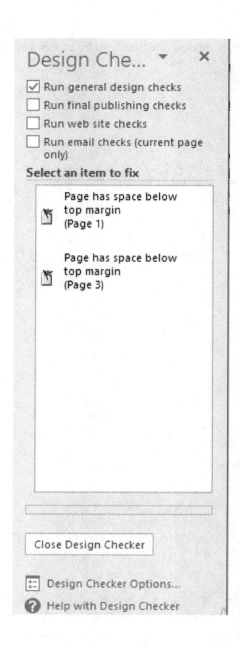

Saving Your Publication

The next thing to do after you have created your Publication is to save it so that you can locate it anytime on your computer. Kindly follow the steps below to save your publication in PDF format.

1. **Click the file tab.**

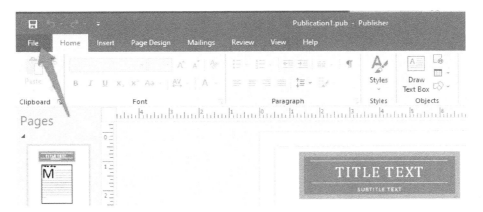

2. **Select Save As from the left-hand side of the screen.**

3. **Choose This PC and select the document.**

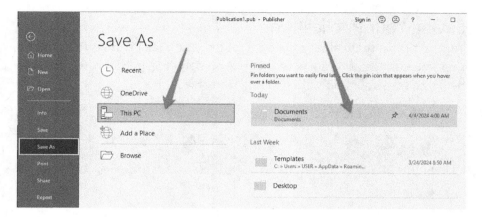

The Save as dialog box appears.

4. Give your document a descriptive name in the File name box.

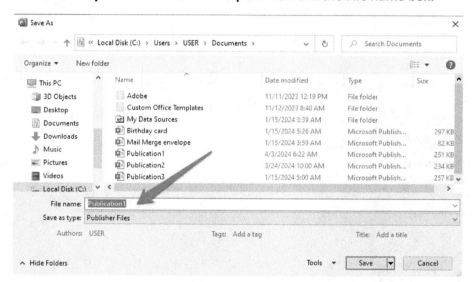

5. On the Save as type click the little arrow to select PDF.

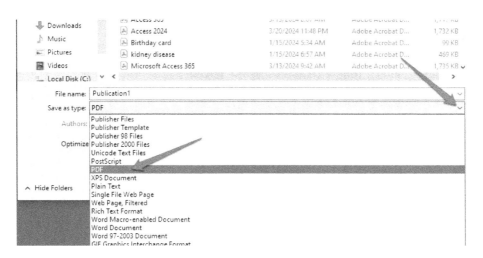

6. Then click the Save button.

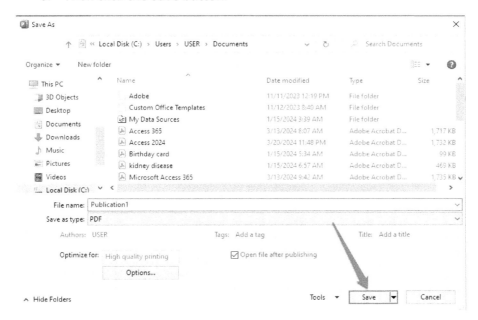

81

Printing a Publication

The final thing to do after you have created and saved your publication is to print it, kindly follow the steps below to print your publication.

1. Click the File tab.

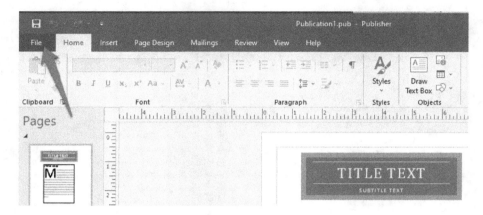

2. Choose Print.

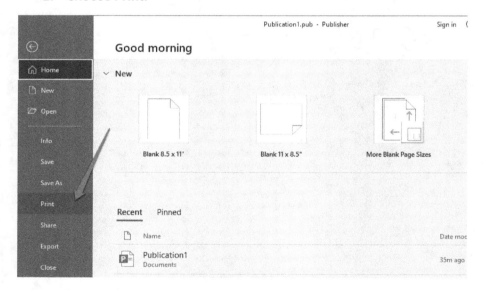

The Print window appears.

3.   Negotiate the Print window and click the Print button.

CONCLUSION

After you have gone through the content in this mini-book I am so sure that you can now make use of Publisher perfectly. I am also certain that you can discover how to create a Publication, redesign a Publication, obtain a better view of your work, enter text on the pages and also make the text fit in text frames, make text wrap around a frame or image, save your publication, printing your publication, and so on.